TRAJECTORIES

SAM EISENSTEIN

TRAJECTORIES

EYEWEAR PUBLISHING

POEMS SELECTED BY
TODD SWIFT
& KELLY DAVIO

First published in 2016
by Eyewear Publishing Ltd
Suite 333, 19-21 Crawford Street
Marylebone, London W1H 1PJ
United Kingdom

Cover design and typeset by Edwin Smet
Author photograph by Chana Ellen Eisenstein DVM
Printed in England by TJ International Ltd, Padstow, Cornwall

ISBN 978-1-911335-25-2

Eyewear wishes to thank Jonathan Wonham for his
generous patronage of our press.

At the author's request, this edition follows American spelling and
usage wherever practicable.

WWW.EYEWEARPUBLISHING.COM

Sam Eisenstein was born in
Bakersfield, California, in
1932. He studied Jungian
Psychology in Zürich and
worked for many years as
a teacher and consulting
therapist. He is the author of
many novels and collections
of short stories. He lives with
his wife in a house crammed
with mechanical toys and
paintings by Outsider artists.
He has been writing poems
for decades, but this is his
debut collection.

Table of Contents

III

IV

I

A Set of My Images

Someone has a set
of my images
nailed to a calendar

Fanning it so that
I appear to move
with the decades
decaying and excusing

Backing up doesn't
blot smudge marks
forward again produces
an entirely different face

Lost between
is a being
who may be me

A printed circuit
3D technology
or minimal stereo

Anxiety about a title
alters the content
even more than surgery

Furor as the image bleeds
through the cassette
onto the lap of the artist

He picks up a phone
even though
anxiety feels like hokum

Asking: are you still alive?
Need a Band-Aid?
Hydration? Rewind?

Try not to slump so
face to chest
wet your lips a little
We're almost there

Born In 1932

Born in 1932
just in time to be deported
to the east

If parents hadn't emigrated
blind to suffering
that waited in the New World

Hating their shared past
in a present shuttered
against Christly hostility

Hoping the children
will understand for them
the ins and outs

I read the works
of survivors
counting the days
of their lives

The return from transport
slaughtered relatives
butchered friends

Image of myself left sprawled
not having resisted
beatings, the heat, cold, starvation

Survival envy not guilt
I carry like a loaded gun
aimed at myself

Hauled before a tribunal
of silent dead
that demands: what have you done
with your life
to merit life?

An accident of geography
allows for both digestion
and placid graduation

Acid flowing from unmarked graves
translates to numbers
this or that one my age
younger or older

Their history is what I covet
without the history
the scars

How they survived
translation by editors
who homogenized suffering

So that their past not like
a book bomb
to explode in my face

Father's Birthday

Once again
as every year
my father's birthday

March in Jewish Bucharest
beginning the 20th century
dreading Christian holydays

That celebrate their savior
protecting him from Jews
with knife and fire

Father learned to walk
softly and almost invisible
as he boarded the ship

That sailed him to me
potential as ripples
receptacle for the pain

Unexpunged by insults
newly inflicted
in the new land

He poured onto me
every unreturned blow
unrealized dream

I was his Jew
He was my gentile
with a clenched fist

Nothing really personal
I was stamped from clay
not even fired

A blurry child
from his weak loins
bound to fail like him

Even if he had to push
and rip the envelope
to stop its growth

Smoke encircled his head
as he decried my tears
even as he caused them

He jeered my average feet
my running nose
my labored breathing

I now really believe
he wanted to care
but the bullies of his youth

Attacked him
wherever he was
forcing him to torture me

Apricots

My mother cultivated them
as much or as little
as she did anything

Including me
whose parental soil
was acid

Yet every year
we fruited
each in our own way

Spotted and irregular
certainly non-commercial
lumpy not sweet

She swept our leaves
with angry energy
refusing fertilizer

Threatening the final cut
not just a pruning
for bad behavior

The innocent tree and me
we were always blamed
for the errant ways

Of weather
absent customers
anti-Semitic neighbors

Father's slack ambition
sister's lack of beaux
peeling paint

Along with growing pain
in breast and groin
the ripening fruit

Mocked her industry
her lack of complaint
in the face of the failure

Of every medication in which
she held some hope
for the easing of pain

The possibility of happiness
probably never crossed
her mind

Yet at least her son might
have taken the time
to admire her a little

Exclaimed over her crop
of apricots
or thanked her while eating

But unconscious of her labor
as of her stoic commitment
while disease ate her alive

I paid no more attention
to her than to the tree
left behind years before

By Her Own Hand

I wonder about her
the one I married
while I was still a boy

Brilliant and wised up
beyond her years
believer in free love

True successor to her elders
stalwart communist cadre
barricaded in a Glendale duplex

Already a bit bent
at fifteen she flashed
saggy tits

For amusement
at an entranced boy
blinded by the glory

who rubbed a hole
in my old car's windshield
week after week

I hunted cannibal aliens
under beds and in closets
while she cowered

Afraid I didn't possess strength
to wrestle them
for possession of her soul

And she was right
my grip loosened
she was borne away

Up into the clouds
where white-coated angels
issued unassailable dicta

Pronounced cured
she disembarked
at the end of a rainbow

Whose dazzle
colored her life
from then to the end

Which began soon
thereafter with tiny shocks
one after another

Almost unfelt
synapses unclasped
bowed their little heads

While far away
in another life
I wondered what marvels

Were commencing
from her teeming mind
so much fuller

Than the poor one
I called my own
tortoise-like shell

Then she was gone
by her own hand
was it bitter disillusion

Did she ever stop
to wonder what if
there had continued
an us?

A Wedding Band

A wedding band
is very loud
from far off

Drums heard foremost
only later flutes
silvery trilling

Fingers faster than
hummingbirds
ply instruments

Legs scissor
like military
heads head forward

A Cracker-Jack box
ring makes music
loud as diamonds

My band adorned
some other finger
now dead or suborned

Water first purled
over magma
shot with gold

In a furnace yielding
running liquid
shed its carapace

An artist fashioned the circle
closed with flesh
sealed with promise

The sun glints on
the passing brassy band
as though on a single ring

Marching down the years
to the time my ring
fuses to bone

While the band plays taps
my ring melts with flesh
again at one with earth

Prelude

I could never have imagined
I would want to forget you,
erase your memory, scent,

Consign every aspect of you
to a neutral holding area
where our fixed connection

May rust and dissolve like iron
in the earth where we both lie
another day, sooner or later,

Having taken with us our loves,
not yours and mine, later ones,
more important to the lives

We lived away from one another,
having quit the dry lightning
of our two personas' upheavals.

Not complementary, more twins
than lovers, fiercely dedicated
to overcoming, never joining.

Your storied body eluded mine,
it demanded poetry, not news,
I wanted only to shoot off words

Into a world inured of sweetness,
which was your essence, unfeigned,
I wanted only to break things.

Now that you are finally dead
I can allow myself to long for you,
allow your presence to come alive

Without a jittery lingering fear
of being overwhelmed, nullified
by your greater specific gravity,

Your way of casual demolition
of casuistry, puerile notions,
even of unmentionable writers.

I could have boarded a plane,
not even for a lot of money
to learn what years had done,

Undone, with your spiny core,
that unyielding stubborn pride
always scorning easy success,

Even access to a greater world
to you always the lesser,
which nonetheless ground you,

Beat on you until you cracked,
even you, adamantine, steely,
the most sphinx-like woman,

Eroded like ancient beliefs
until only the husk remained,
idol-like, still refusing to give in,

Choosing finally the finality
of a mortal potion administered
by yourself, no other qualified.

The Chosen

A thin old lady who exercises
lifting weights

protrudes the tip of her tongue
from a corner of her mouth
demonstrating the concentration

she surely demonstrated
lifting rocks at Mauthausen quarry
eight, ten daily trips up
and down the 'stairway of death'

her mirror-like blue eyes conceal any clue
to the miracle of her survival

how she stored energy enough
to meet the gaze
of a prisoner toiling in the other direction

in the tiny moment that promises were made
she received strength to keep living

as each new day she dreaded
he had been pushed into the chasm by merry guards

'I was the one.' he told her, after liberation
She was never really sure
but accepted his declaration

and lived with him for fifty years

An Ageing Couple

To see one of them
tenderly holding the elbow
of the other guiding him
to the next machine
is to sense the depth and
length of their association

The one leading wears an awry toupee
of which the other probably is not aware
as the last he saw anything of the world
was long before

War? Accident? Diabetes?
Maybe he can forget
while pumping the bike
to country western music
favored by the head nurse

Two bulky ageing men
all their history written on the hand
tendered on the other's elbow

Almost achingly familiar
this naked gesture
enacted before all of us
atop our devices

Reminding us
as valves arteries
pumps whir and gasp
of our hope that what kills
doesn't first take pieces

What Is Left

What can you leave
when you don't believe
in the after-life?

Little post-it notes
to the accidental sweeper
that may stop him or her

A moment before dumping
the work of a lifetime
of sweaty hours

Poring over thesaurus
and faded snapshots
fervent letters

Of forgotten relationships
not to call them affairs
certainly not friendships

Looking for the key
to instant popularity
or least some recognition

Before all the joints
decide to freeze
along with neurons

The unpublished items
singular insights
so much stronger

Than much-quoted
merely trivial
utterances of fools

In the public eye
lucky with their friends
or when they were born

Blessed with offspring
who will cherish
that which is stashed

Here and there
like an Easter egg hunt
with profound treasures

That will blow their brains
inaugurate a new era
cause monuments' erection

Or not
but at least remain
not compressed or burned

Why should I care?
Words warmed me
even those not incendiary

Surrounded me like walls
to keep out noise
and popular trash

Kept me humble
staving off popularity
not caving to lies

Following a trend
this or that irony
straining after the next thing

Though to tell the truth
I would have traded honesty
for the big bucks

At least to leave
the kids something
they can sell

They're All Dead

They're all dead
and you don't miss them
except at sunset

When wisps of cloud
punctuate the blushing
horizon

Or the refrain
of an old song seeps
out of a window

A sticky something
wouldn't detach itself
from a shoe

During first walk
with a girl
who became
wife then corpse

Wobbling upstage
became a clown's walk
ending a career

Giggling sex
on the beach
dribbled sand
into every wrong place

All gone to dust
the play's hero
that stage itself

Even memory dies
as the emulsion of photos
adheres to one another

In incoherent embrace
as though necessity
to confuse then crumble

Over-rides every
recollection, embrace
loving or angry word

Synapses bow low
turn their backs
and vanish
along with their images

Of every body
taste, sight
the world entire

Ulysses' Gaze

It's coming, by post, by air and land,
a piece of music that I dread hearing,
because it recalls innocents slaughtered,

In a mist that hides from assailants
as well as their victims the terrible truth,
that murder is easier as it recurs.

Neighbors have no problem slitting
the throats of whoever's designated
their eternal mortal enemies,

That is, until the armistice, peace at last,
broken glass swept up and away,
severed limbs buried and forgotten.

After a generation even the murdered
forget their graves and names,
a frail grandchild shrugs her shoulder.

But music, like a fingernail on blackboard,
insists that your spine resonate
even if memory doesn't care.

A figure rises from a body still warm,
unable to make the terrible noise
that will alert animals in the woods,

Cause them to flee, why they know not,
but horror passes the species barrier,
even while memory stays behind.

Why do I insist on hearing it again?
Both composer and film-maker are dead,
their lists of accomplishments already vague,

As even the most remembered are lost,
after gossip and the tawdry disappear,
even the holiest and most revered.

Where did this music come from?
Did the composer suffer enough
to write it down without bleeding,

Through the stylus, the keys, the audio,
so immense the wailing, it comes across
years and continents and languages?

It is music that is utterly silent,
its tones coming from reverberations
of memories not at all tonal,

Music that forces strangers to clasp
trembling fingers hoping not to fall prey
to the stranger who wishes their ends,

The fanatic whose one sharp deed
was to force blood from a child,
from a new mother, whose joy,

Cut short in a gurgle of sliced breath,
gives birth to a terrible sweetness
vented by an innocent orchestra.

I'm Just Fine

A smashed hand
a little child
holds it outstretched
like a ghastly bouquet

If staring out at me
from the photo
can change destiny
keep looking

Though a child doesn't know
the word can't think past
the bulb of unrecognizable bloom
that was his or her hand

See, I can't even discern
the gender of the hand
that might later
have held in its grip
the fruit of another's body

Sensitive brush of flesh
against whorl
or actual plucking of a flower
along a curb
as a child is urban

In the countryside
few homes collapsed
with the blind weight
of masonry against flesh

Flesh itself shuddered away
not quickly enough
to prevent forever loss
of feeling, tone, shape

Not flattened, not so much
but enough to cause shock
a look of dismay, disbelief

Somehow even disdain
that something so unbelievable
unreal could intrude
in such a short life

What can destiny perform
with a return bout
all of life used up like that
nothing left for the octogenarian

Except anonymous lines
in that same flattened palm
wrinkles as of a life well-lived
not used up before
it was well begun.

How am I feeling? Fine,
I didn't live there
my block wasn't crushed.
I live far beyond the horrid cries.

Homegrown Hero

The car ahead of mine
burst into noisy flames flinging
debris across four lanes

Hardly waiting for the brakes
to take screeching hold
I flung myself into the maelstrom

The toddler wobbled into lanes
forgetting my torn tendon
I grabbed him shuddering

Aware I would become
paste on the bumper
of the next car

Looking beseeching up
at the god-like cloud
I cut a deal with death

For gratitude I pressed
my anti-incoming missile
deflector knowing full well

Radiation would kill me
within only a few days
with which to write

A screed that will change
all hate into love
however transient

While squeezing spinsters
into holy matrimony
albeit with unworthy males

Nothing so wonderfully zany
ever transpires in my dullard
life of little occasion

Nonetheless, I take credit
for unlikely salvations
because I was willing

Thus I plan to plant a bomb
in a hated colleague's car
to become supreme enabler

His demise will elevate me
selling newspapers on track
to become extinct as dodos

Prevent the widow
from losing her annuity
she can pay for the child's goiter

Incite the government
to demand more safeguards
against homegrown heroes

Eternity

If I avoid this crack
I will live untold years
in splendid health

My parents will have been
wealthy if unobtrusive
with their largesse

My sister will have kissed
the swollen bruise
magically disappearing it

Auschwitz will have been
a summer camp for cripples
dedicated to restoration

Al Dreyfus became president
of a protestant France
bowing to erection

Of monuments to Huguenots
who taught the nation
divine tolerance

I will keep genes
of passion for canines
for my own use

Not simply pass them on
to ungrateful progeny
who have forgotten me

Almost before I leave
this frenetic stage
wherein they act

As though no parent
ever touched them
in their innermost

Though to be fair
I myself did so
as soon as ever possible

Folk where I work
settle on me
the role of elder

Cherish every word even
the swish of my garments
the subject of paeans

If I avoid this crack
my tree-dwelling forebears
will forebear to invent

Religion and its tools
to ensure compliance
by way of torture

My years of perfected health
will have purpose
beyond my little ego

Also nothing else will die
the world will impact
there will be no more food

But no one will complain
life alone is worth starvation
everyone will agree

And also to hurl me
into the chasm
where originated that crack

II

Early Blooms

Early blooming flowers
get their pollinating done
before fatigue sets in

Even insects need rest
away from their duties
bringing nectar to the nest

They spread their petals
with arrogant aplomb
their next generation settled

Like humans who've sent
offspring to college
sandwiches packed and ready

We also are impatient
to ripen to fertilization
misconstrued as maturity

With gaudy celebrations
in tribal codes
denoting availability

Untouched flowers wither
disappointing their species
also moms and dads

Labeled as wallflowers
they disappear unnoticed
unheralded barrens

Early birds pounce
do what nature requires
which is to reproduce

As human children
we hope to hasten
signs of readiness

Eager bosoms
ancillary hair
steely handshake

Not wanting to notice
that early flowering
becomes speedy withering

Last Chance

'I'm hoping to have a last affair with an interesting, ambulatory, 75–80-year-old Westchester man.' – New York Review of Books, January 12, 2012

Ambulatory and ambulance
share a scary root
last and lasting

Are contradictory
likely her Westchester
a boring neighborhood

Is in New York
not a dreary LA suburb
where nothing happens

That last affair thing
makes me nervous
as in daggers and last will

And testament
is she after my retirement
is she herself ambulatory

In excess as in hyperactive
or was she a courtesan
for all her previous years

As in how old
is she anyhow
and what constitutes

Interesting is it handball
bowling, mahjong, tennis?
Or bar stool flying?

She advertises in a bookish
publication dedicated to thought
does she have a will to power

Is it Nietzsche or Schopenhauer
that turns her on
Poe, one of the James brothers

So many imponderables
like will she require
nightly ballroom visits

Does she floss regularly
or plunk her teeth in a glass
how much weight does her bra

Need to bear
how about ex mates
are they lurking near?

Hope is next to superstition
are you a born-again
votary of one or another sect?

All the other ads flaunt slender,
sleek, charming, rollicking
foxy and passionate

But you only want a last affair
is it cancer that makes you
so somber and serious?

Fore-knowledge of an apocalypse
pending in Westchester, NY
but not in Westchester, LA

This may be my last chance
to participate
in her last affair

Opportunity beckons but once
I'll close my eyes
and leap into the void

Inevitability

I've met the one I'm meant to marry,
not so immediately, but ultimately,
I haven't much to say about it,

But my dog knows and doesn't like it,
he refuses to meet her caring gaze
when we chance to meet almost daily,

He won't accept gradual departure
of his beloved mistress care-giver,
her fierce desire to stay alive, here,

Not accepting any end as inevitable,
a belief I try desperately to abet
with medicine, doctors, voodoo,

All to some avail, not nearly enough
to keep the reaper from our field,
and her hot anger from erupting

Like a lava flow in unlikely places,
followed by apologies for outbreaks
from the constant pain she endures.

The younger one, who feeds rabbits
and other unattractive varmints,
would likewise like to feed me,

Moves almost lasciviously sans bra,
never obvious, but so clearly mine,
the dog wants to bite her ankle,

Also naked and unafraid of sight,
as are her lips, palely painted,
but the whole package is just that,

Waiting only for the address label,
my name and station in life,
a larger rabbit ready for its cage.

The Ad Not Taken

She wants me to move
to her side of the continent
with nothing but my breath

From my old stale life
of careful indoctrination
pedestrian as a flu shot

Go naked and unashamed
she urges as sibilant
as wind horizontal

In a wildly clangorous
treetop dropping fruit
instantly to produce drunken

Stupor in which dream
of her unknown face
glitters like constellations

Unobscured by columns
of other urging ads
she shines like shook foil

Since I cannot come
to an easy term for intoxication
and must borrow

While I temporize, delay
because at this point in life
such a move cannot be removed

I am to be a book flinging itself
onto a bonfire of inanities
seeking a clean burn

Wondering will I sight her
through the flames
or merely turn to ash?

Will she lure this unwary
to certain destruction
if untied from the mast

Because her words
clench on a throat
tired of its hum

Because she knows
that visualizing starkness
is itself the most seductive

Even if the result is to freeze
while disrobing in flight
intoxicated with presentiment

Her paper ad burns
into my sternum
ejecting other contents

Becomes every book
that advocates rebirth
flight from the sterile

A shudder runs through
my memory mechanism
desperate to retain its hold

As I strain to throw it off
regardless of the danger
to longevity's tenure

I fling the publication
redolent with appeal
into waiting conflagration

Her adorable face
dims and fades
to absent ash

Not So Much Sweethearts

We were not so much sweethearts
as exchanging favors
her body and psych notes
and my promises

Not so much promises
as wise cracks from
intermediate Chaucer

Not so much Chaucer
as my fervent dismissal of
her parents' money

Not money so much
but their bed
that moved every
which way

Not any way leading to love
bodies and minds melding
slick sweat a nuisance

Not so severe a problem
as the thickness
of her glasses

Flashing liquid when she spoke
of our future together
after Psych 101

Of the deep unconscious
connection's bright pathway
to upper class status

When we were mated
and married
that all fell apart
on a drive down Sunset

Among the animated ads
when I announced a future
that did not include her bed
spectacles skin or notes

Thrift Store Ghosts

Thrift store ghosts are easy to invoke,
you only have to try on something,
a dress, a sweater, a chaise lounge.

Hold out ghostly arms to catch one
strolling by in one of the aisles,
lost, in the clutches of after-life,

Not quite ready to yield possession
to the next-in-line bargain-hunter,
as acquiring things was not so easy,

Took sweating at an indifferent job,
weighing something shiny and new
against salting away some money.

Their location is easy to determine,
as a ghostly aura hovers over,
a veritable traffic jam of spirits,

But their presence must be ignored
if you're to find and buy the relics
of those newly dearly departed.

That wedding dress, worn once,
or even maybe more than once,
a little bit damaged, long-treasured.

A sweater, worn to that wedding,
or was it to the funeral of one
with whom she was at odds?

The jumble of kitchen utensils,
so many hands, the ghosts confused
by one another's histories.

There are no ghosts, of course,
only ones we must manufacture
because history is essential,

Mythology part and parcel of living,
the dead provide us with book ends
to secure us in our necessity to buy

Into their slow or hasty departures
in the atmosphere of thrift shops,
where almost everything finally lands.

Film Versus Digital

I prefer film to pixels
as one way of staving off
encroaching age

Which overwhelms
no matter which
technology is utilized

But with film
it can be micromanaged
through the lapse

Of time it takes
to develop and grasp
the latent image

Which through the delay
has changed only slightly
but enough

To encourage a feeling
of control over
the ambient world

Some mastery over time
disease, the overthrow
of both dictator and democrat

Mystery and expectation
of what film will reveal
not known at the moment
of exposure

Latency that every growth
needs to mature
pertains to film

But not to pixels
wholly automatic
robotic inhumane

Like instant coffee
or freeze-dried food
just as tasteless

March 3, 1903

My father was born
in a stark bare
wooden room

Squeezed from generations
of similar scenarios
of Jewish peasantry

Stock footage shows
bristling beards
hands buried in aprons

Nowhere in view
are eyes I can
look into for community

Or kinship with books
music or paint
travel to snow and sand

The woman that bore him
receded immediately
into a medieval shtetel

Did she ever cradle
the premature old man
born with white hair

Dentures and pot belly
who even as an infant
frowned at me
with automatic disapproval

My father looks back
from the vantage point
of one hundred eight years

Ruminates over the passage
of time that evens
out the generations

Tries to remember
whose faces grace
faded photos pasted
into tattered books

As my daughter may look
back on me in a future
secured by pixels

Wondering who I was
at my birth bald
and bearded

As mystified and pained
by her father as I was
by mine

Grown Up

I liked it better
when you were irrational
and I was the voice of reason

If only you had stayed
three and howling
when your tummy hurt

Placated with a promise
of instant gratification
the only signal of love

I don't care
for such reversal
it hurts my tummy

How well you learned
how to translate
the language of hurt

That bubbles from below
toppling all the blocks
in a juvenile rage

Into calm surveillance
of a landscape of craving
that cries, look at me

How I suffer
from being suffered
but not celebrated

Your hand on my shoulder
that used to clutch it
urging calm

I pretend to resist
the maturity that I
helped to create

Grateful for that reservoir
of better sense
that I now tap

The Messages

I know why she doesn't delete
messages from her Mom and me

We already were old when she was young,
embarrassments at parents' night:
'are those your grandparents?'

Stay-at-homes while others camped, skied,
shucked ball and bat
or feigned enthusiasm for sleep-overs

Evening the score, her mother created
the neatest Hallowe'en costumes
planned stunning parties on her birthday
knew when to cuddle
when things didn't go as planned

When to leave her alone by the fish pond
to ponder
the mystery of who she will
become

As she matured we grew younger
until we speak from the same height

Often
it can be casual hello or shock
when a friend or another parent dies

She wants our voices
in her ears
as when

We were alive
our arms around her shoulders
our lips on her cheeks

Love Poem

Long ago neighbors
sat somber
in our living room

To inform us primly
they could no longer
be friends

Because we bickered
all the time
they suffered

Our daughter winced
at our shouting matches
threats of separation

The current dog
was the single object
worth staying for

Years passed
accreting feelings
at so minimal a rate

As to be almost invisible
imperceptibly
we closed gaps

Illnesses helped
the possibility of losing
the other

Made real the void
life would become
without that sensibility

The enduring mystery
of magnetic attraction
invisible inevitability

That brought us together
in the first bonding
emotion like molasses

Now in old age renders us
to be almost each other
grown into one

While that chiding couple?
They divided their names
eons ago

III

A Bland Snorkeler

Who am I
after nearly eight decades
of falling in the same direction

Like a series of dominoes
so fast
space between them
blurs

A mosquito might pry
apart
for any blood

Circumcision's drop
stands for the whole
as it thins

Lengthening to the scar
of a by-pass
after the by-blow

Asking what-if
how old would I be
if you had let me

Maybe dead
in a forgotten battle
or amputee
equally unpronounced

Dominoes clammy as sweat-
stained underwear
stick together

The way families
are supposed to
refusing to give up

Secrets of decades
past
fused by memory's
vagaries

Into a geological flesh
no more salient
than topography

Like coral
visible only as a corpse
I join ancestors

Watching if such a thing
were possible
a bland snorkeler
from the future

Featureless

The pool contains multitudes
as well as those hanging from limbs
uneasy above whirlpools

That lead to featureless
multipotent present time
far in an unfathomable future

And the company they keep
willy-nilly via genome
and continental drift

Those religious forebears
loathe distant progeny
who sneer at their naïveté

Scholars watch terrified
by daredevil revolutionaries
seeking overthrow

Of whatever's in place
in favor of the untried
rainbow blush of the new

In my dream delirium
I snatch at life with both hands
trying to stay out of the way

Of my rioting blood
segments of which
earnestly seek to exterminate

Any molecules in disagreement
of their particular tribal
racial and cultural origins

Whether savanna, leafy
arboreal, maritime
or lodged in caves

Every cell murderous
in its passion to prevail
over divergence

May allow foreign growth
to take mortal root
as an almost suicidal turn

Of the cellular shoulder
all or nothing it hisses
engulfed and snuffed

Stop, I cry, half-awakening
knowing the dream prophetic
I am at peace with all of you

Knowing this a conscious lie
as impossible as immortality
except for the invader

I can only urge the dream
to take the direction of reconciliation
a kind of united nations

Enough time to produce
another generation
perhaps wiser than mine

Being Seventy-Nine

Being seventy-nine
a tick away from decade
ninety and the yawning

Abyss beyond
where wisps of smoke
mark final fire

Finished worries over joints
that creak and crack
or the necessity of
too many flushes

Bitterness over
so many items taken
for granted in life
running hopping

Jumping, stooping
never wondering
if one will rise again

To look someone
in the eyes without
regret for mouth

Without wrinkles
or to hide missing teeth
cracked lips

For narrative
not dependent on notes
or straining for continuity

Ninety used to be only
a speedometer reading
not an ambush

Of friends and enemies
peeled like banana skins
leaving frail fruit

For time to continue
to bite with fierce teeth
growing frailty

How nature jeers
flaunting newly-minted
rosy flesh against flesh

While mine mines
only the pillow
with a gratitude unknown

To blithe uncaring
fertile bodies that swing
ahead and behind

Almost touching
yet years apart
and I invisible

The Banana

Beyond counting
the number of bananas
I've ruthlessly stripped

The present one
suddenly stands out in light
of a slight case of melanoma

Even to undergo
a small patch
of epidermis stripped

Call it peel or skin
it shields the delicate
body within

Despite absurdity
I become this banana
flayed raw

No pathetic fallacy
neither pathetic
nor fallacious

I am willy-nilly
this banana
mutely naked

What of the pitting
of peach or apricot
fruit's inner essence

Yawning vacancy
sudden absenting
of all its future

Does grass
sense gnashing blade
and gird its loins

Envisioning savannahs
progeny without number
grazing cattle

Finally able to comprehend
religious apology
upon taking life

I attempt to be
in some small way
a banana

Squirrel, Drowned

While Betty prepared yams
exactly the precise amount
of sugar to rum

Dead turkey ruminated
at least as much
as ever it did in life

I thought of the squirrels
playing high above
rushing branch to branch

Chasing a sexual thing
or simply plenitude of life
exuberant energy

At a moment of cooking
spoonful of this or that
squinting at a gauge

The squirrel missed his footing
and fell into the pool
and went down and down

In his little mind
was this just a continuation
of his species' way of play?

A moment then to emerge
laughing the way squirrels do
in high-pitched excitement?

But he continued going down
and eventually drowned
his little mind winked out

While the playmate above
waited for the next round
flicking her tail provocatively

Simply annoyed or anxious
or making ready for the next
or just what?

Items we killed or plucked
are passive in the pan
like forks and knives

After extensive play
or furious work
we find ourselves

At the bottom of a pool
one last moment
looking up to the light

Resignation

Retirement means
it's time
to replace the tires

Worn out with spinning
their wheels
over countless revolutions

An other meaning's retreat
from battle
giving over and up

Some other revolution
could even signify
freedom from the spurious

Humdrum everyday turn
of the sun
on the same dull patch

Of road and job
repeated dull signals
from an ageing gut

The spark plugs
no longer so sparkling
the inner tube gone

The way of the dodo
as flightless as an old
typewriter or carbon paper

So: at the very least
allow the tired tire
to become a swing

To bear the exultant
bodies of the young
and as yet thoughtless

Students

Students walk the halls
each ruminating on
his or her terrors

Of being alone forever
always being behind
in some obligation

Having forgotten to read
the assignment
or neglected it

For momentary distraction
against illness
or memory of infidelity

Fumbling hands in the dark
enforced silences
permanent humiliation

Professor's airy demands
for yet another text
of his own authorship

The sense of being
no more than one digit
in a computer

How language
can be a coiled snake
waiting to strike

No matter how prepared
how prayerful
or slinky-eyed

If brokers cheat
and favorite rock stars
your father too

Why not you
to get ahead
pass the course

Escape these halls
deadly requirements
the roll call

Stale bed clothes
numbing hours of work
public transportation

For endless love
ideal fulfillment
with a mate who's liquid

Whose dip into your bosom
flushes a wedding bouquet
and a reliable used car

The skeletons of all those
walking the halls
look very much alike

To the observing fates
whose rules require
a certain percentage

Be sacrificed
to accident
regardless of virtue

Classless Reunion

It was sixth in a series
spanning the decades
since we graduated

Half of us are dead
printed neatly in two columns
like soldiers' graves

We are united
in the dining room
of a country club

Where as teenagers
blacks and Jews among us
were unspokenly not welcome

Now served food
unpalatable as
management
can manage

Since before the first decade
was ended
the only two people
dear to me were gone

Nobody I asked
could say how
nor cared as they had been
also outside looking in

I resisted querying
of my first real girlfriend
how we managed
the gear shift

Retired from being a principal
and pillar of her church
urging total abstinence

The richest kid
the only other Jew
never invited me to swim

As my family
had no standing
wore shabby clothing
shame to the community

Now in our eighth decade
equality settles on our shoulders
shapeless waists
and sunken cheeks

We are athletes
in a slow race
panting to outdistance
the other few living

To the final reunion
of eight hundred
who started as sprinters

Become eight sets
of eyes guttering
around one table

Here Comes Eternity

I have been rewarded
for admiring many
of the greatest culture heroes

With the ability
to penetrate other universes
and even manipulate them

To change the one
from which I emanate
however I want

Mahler not dead at fifty
Einstein's aneurysm gone
Roosevelt's heart intact

Going into the 18th century
the too many tracks
make for confusion

Alas for Mozart, Schumann,
Mendelssohn, Stendhal
or ancestors

Who yearned to observe
their seed achieve majority
not early cut down

By vicious followers
of the Jew Jesus
who himself punctured

Though his singlehood
is not enough-established
nor can I solve that one

Disaffection

Breath won't congeal
on a window
tracing a heart pierced
by an arrow
isn't optional

A well-defined
pair of buttocks
inspires nostalgia
not so much desire

A turn to view
a child squirming on some
young lap or shoulder
wounds the ribs

A sort of fog
obscures objects
of charity

Distance becomes inverse
to real space
as mirrors are peopled
by far-off crowds

A kind of tinnitus
afflicts hearing
when requested
for contact

Preview of the great void
rehearsal for curtain closing
relaxes the grip
of various organs

Tears that can't heal
hasten dissolution
lessen pain

Taking off
one jettisons
accustomed weight
in return for free transit

Celebration of Life Events For

Fax announcement pops up in the machine
on top of a breathless announcement for re-fi
and half-price drapes/take-down cleaning and resizing

Throwing away the others I take the letter-size paper
decorated around all the corners
with cactus and happy-face butterflies
to the kitchen with a cold half-empty coffee cup

Tip-toeing around still-sleeping wife exhausted
from arranging the estate
of my dead high school English teacher
who left no instruction

Because she simply wasn't ready to die before her cat
religious-stubborn challenged god to take her off-side
she blew the whistle on him
as she had for junior varsity girl basketball

Rinse my favorite cup imprinted with cats and dogs
shedding fleas as it's heated
prop the announcement on the coffee machine

Take out fruit, bread and eggs and boil water for tea
squint at the weather
having forgotten my glasses
as I plucked the coffee cup

The dog is ready for first of four walks
around the block
he'll take more if I forget the count
I'm encouraged to misplace

The gardener has neglected to repot the dahlia
I must remind my wife who will be annoyed
at the loss of a bulb, not cheap

Another crack in the ceiling
from a too-small-to-be-noticed earthquake
the paint's chipped behind the toaster
from too-frequent heating

His life reduced to a series of hyphens
Brandon is electrons buzzing through fax
Viewing: Service: Internment

Grammatical mischance more accurate than trajectory
of the life

The weather clearing up
I'll be able to read the paper outside

Birthday At Eighty

No agreement
at least tacit
even a coupon

You could brandish
in mornings
hard to bend over

20% off your age
would be something
you'd eagerly agree to

Portions are slimmer
the menu blander
lacking illumination

But dining at all
much better than
being dined upon

Candles on the cake
by general agreement
remain symbolic

Presents are demure
offerings of gratitude
from the younger

Tending to large print
casual garments
and stout sticks

For fending off
gypsies and stray dogs
eager insurance agents

Most agreeable
to make comfortable
your remaining minutes

So long as ample reward
is at hand
from your shaky signature

Even if precocious vision
foresaw what was to come
agreement with your body

Wasn't worth the parchment
as it is the most duplicitous
crawling thing on the planet

Prey to every malaise
from top to bottom
especially the bottom

Ergo embarrassment
at the party
a discreet packet

A joke gift not funny
at an age at which
night frights are real

So many generations
have arisen since yours
they crowd your sight

Which can be mistaken
merely a flock of sheep
or your parents beckoning

IV

In Love With Sled Dogs

I fell in love with the sled dogs
while waiting for an x-ray
of varicosed veins

Blood pressure having soared
beyond any reasonable horizon
watching the frozen tundra

Loosened as temperatures soared
crackling with walruses
baying their need

For winter carcasses
in ample supply
what with global warming

Because they exist
only on a DVD
my instant love not reciprocated

A happy ending was expected
as the film came out of Disney

I do fall in love
stumble into passion
or empathic tears

Even with strange
dogs I do not know
from walks around the block

Where does such feeling come from?
How does a feeling like this help
my genes leap their boundaries

To find a home
in the next generation?
Surely not with sled dogs

Even Disney can't keep
the natural from being drowned
by the power
of religious morons

Hyperventilation

We dribble in to cardiac rehab
some limping others with canes
our histories trailing us

Like toilet paper stuck
to shoes and sandals
invisible to us

But pretty obvious
to the rest of the crew
softly hyperventilating

On various vicious machines
meant to mock our debilities
with cheery names like 'Schwinn'

T-shirts advertise our affinities
pathetic desires to triumph
over age, valve failure

Multiple deaths
spouse and vigor
an age which we've outlived

Into the bewilderment
of faster angrier machinery
of bewildering complexity

One sports a Bengal tiger
another a set of giraffes
or a growling NRA boast

Of protecting America
allowing everyone the choice
of whom to shoot

All united in desperation
to reach the next birthday
even with chocolate prohibited

Nobody knows wherefore
compulsion is built-in
like a spreading waist

Disappearance of the gluteal
in men sagging of the rest
in female cohorts

Yet the atmosphere is one
of cheer and jollity
of going it together

In this room
time is stopped
for an hour

Arid retirement
reversed by a cheery nurse
taking blood pressures

As though they are
more important measurements
than the stock market

And so they are
in this hermetic resort
like ageing molecules

We swirl almost dancing
so happy to obey
what the doctors ordered

Lab Protocol

I wear a slightly-bloodied cotton ball
as proof I possess health insurance
which doesn't insure health

Or even assurance the test
tests anything useful
like for a tumor, obscured
artery, rampant old-age

Neither do they locate passion
or palpate ancient love
regret another specialty
altogether

Requiring separate OK
from the insurance company's
head office

Fear in the waiting room
settles like a dust cloud
fills my lungs
obscures vision

Nobody here is young
except for the obese
sounded for survival
after removal of handfuls of intestine

Who soulfully pine for a future
of bone-prodding bikinis
and ogling eyes

My desire more modest
I want only to stay in one piece
for awhile
to oversee my dog's old age
be buried with him
in a single container

Entertain my daughter's lovers
with cranky stories
made up for the occasion

Give my wife occasion
to make lists of my meds
as she no longer has need to monitor
my comings and goings

The tech's glance rolls down my cheeks
like tears
I am no more than skin to be pierced

Before lunch
where finally, finally
something good may happen

Unsung Heroes of The Race

Obsolete technologies
like the little toe
and vermiform appendix

Should occupy hallowed places
like superseded memories
buried by later events

With what girlfriend
did I slouch at Bob's Big Boy
discussing what?

The agony of dissolution
has itself dissolved
leaving not a groan

Ontogeny recapitulates Phylogeny
insists our gill slits
and furry paws

Served living function
proving even partial truth
can be built on

Pillars mired in shadows
of forgotten events
are what formed me

We who stand
on the shoulders
of pygmies

Salute the tape deck
disparaged parent
of the VCR

Eager for immortality
ignorant of bitterness
arriving with certain knowledge

That nature cares only
that the bloom
be fertilized

That an individual flower
fall so a leaf
may parent the twig

Our individual
little identities
are unsustainable

Even the brilliant
must lose their light
passed to the next up

My Doctor

He squints at my malady
a hint of his bow
and arrow youth
my groin the target

As boy explorer
he was taught to sniff
the object of the hunt

Really to uncover
he had to love it
to discover
where it lurked

The sensitive nose
of the native
an acquired trait

Peels away
clothes odors
even skin

Of the target
in his cross hairs
bring it home

My scrotum is
no different
as a study

He holds it
in both hands
stiffly above his head
for the sun

To penetrate
any remaining mystery
never minding

My arched back
blood pooling
in head and toes

As in blushing triumph
he cuts another gash
in his bow

Everywhere Coded Messages

Everywhere coded messages
from the brain's
interiormost places
where a migraine's slash

Is only the beginning
of waves that pound fjords
into precise patterns

Like nettles on a bush
thorns on a rose
ants marching
in exact formation

As only poverty
in our auditory equipment
guards us from hearing
their haunted refrain

As also of trees
whose branches' rustle
reveal only the smallest
part of their story

Sap's pulsing
like Morse Code
as fractals predict
stock market cataclysms

Perfect roundness
in the cheeks of a girl
mirrors her spleen

As well perfection
of her innocent response
to simple questions
of probity, identity, quantity

The secret message
in the tattoo of blood
that madly thuds
where knife makes a path

Which way a flag flaps
predicts war's duration
the exact number of casualties

The blueness
of the cuticles of a sorceress
foretells her charge

Search dim corridors
of image and dream
for even lifetimes

But a lever will not present
itself to shatter to pieces
the subtle clock revealing
within the ultimate
coded message

Any Body

Any body can suffer
slight derangement
of a living part

Go on with play
or serious business
without another thought

Though a miniscule tear
may open the area
to a slow drip

From the hostile outside
easily stoppered
by a superb system

But persistent leaks
produce a flow
that begins to fill

Inviolate compartments
with living walls
unsinkable rooms

Tiny faceless entities
stoke the boilers
to keep alive

Electrical connections
without which
saving light isn't possible

Fluid continues to rise
threatening to overwhelm
the heart's pumps

Unused to frigid water
filled with unfriendly
creatures of another deep

At the very top and forward
the brain is dazed
with contradictory messages

Fight or flight
or both at once
results in stasis

Accidental decisions
may result in suffocation
or a timely rescue

Most often it's the elderly
who drown
in their own secretions

Yet a small silent cut
may be fatal
even to the youthful

The unsinkable body
veers and topples
as all the lights wink out

No Mother

… no mother will grow old or die if her son doesn't kill her…
– Marcel Proust

When she was dying
in the sterile white room
without a single flower

I circled her with camera
snapping many pictures
from every angle

As her tired eyes followed
blinking at every exposure
as though they were blows

By an uncaring enemy
impersonally landing on her
uncomplaining body

She may have seen me
as emissary from mortuary
or an immigration official

Most of her was gone
by the time of the shoot
eaten by cancers

She could have endured
almost anything
but my cold observation

From her only son
she had protected
with her body's warmth

Through all the sickness
endless nights of strain
shallow asthmatic breaths

What did I expect
to take home
on flimsy film

I elected not to grasp
in years of neglect
with irritable notes

The only communication
with her whose only desire
was my happiness

But had no adequate words
to express a silent passion
and so remained mute

To me a sign of dumbness
and filial shame
took the place of love

The shutter clicked
like teeth in a skull
when brain has turned to dust

And regret fills the memory
of that day in the sterile room
lifting the faded photos

To the height they are owed
more gentle than I deserve
honoring her too late

Nursing Home

Walk out of your home
down the familiar sidewalk
avoid the loose cobble

And think as many times
it should be replaced
or someone's going to trip

But it won't be you
as this is the last time
you will walk there

Festivities are over
last belongings packed
reduced to one valise

Like a doll on a shelf
sharing space with photos
and dead insects

For the first time
not free to choose
companions-to-be

Schedule day's events
the kind of diet
even temperature

Smiles will be of the sort
reserved for small children
or the mentally distressed

This is what is called
luck of the draw
to persist as survivor

The only one standing
after the other
remains as a whisper

Wry with your discomfort
the partner always firm
ever decisive

Reduced to counting cobbles
wishing for oblivion
sucking back tears

Obituaries/Funeral Announcements

Invariably portray
with photos
cheery countenances
of those now beyond

Any stuffy truths
or inconvenient facts
that litter their former lives

All of them were great
parents, kids, bosses
in lives cut short

No matter how long
in earthly duration
and tedium of work

Cheery because
now past hideous illness
worry over finances

The awful boredom
of family sympathy
hollow accolades

The photos prove
that after-life exists
as the deceased

Are glad to go
eager for the embrace
of their deity

As well as his mother
uncle, stepfather
assorted angels

Or the fiercely agnostic
glad at the moment
of extinction

To be gathered
with molecules of dust,
Napoleon, the odd mammoth

It's the cheeriness
that convinces me
as I grumble over pain

Featured more prominently
every birthday that grinds
my bones ever more

The way the photos relate
to one another
communicating serenity

Reassurance of the fact
they all elected to go
of their own free will

In which they believe
despite every cancer
or organ failure
to the contrary

No panic widens eyes
in the photos
or bitterness

At being sliced from life
like so much sausage
or flowers cut for bouquet

Their permanent place
with one another
in the daily newspaper

Grants them the eternity
that implacable decay denies

Occult Blood

Bad enough to call me
by my first name
she mispronounces it

I am reduced
to the humble level
of an anonymous

Elderly whose job it is
to meekly trail behind
a starched behind

For which I am
the nth old person
she will endure

Though without me
she lacks employment
no piano lessons

For the next generation
after hers though
as she's still fertile

There's still time
in case of disaster
and who knows

I may be infectious
thus she won't approach
except when necessary

To apply an instrument
to my flabby upper limb
while rapidly chewing

On gum a product
promoted to calm
nerves about to pop

After a dull day of stale
sour-smelling elders
who shuffle

And refuse to die
of some cryptogenic ill
or leak of occult blood

Outside this office
from some orifice
or electric failure

Oh, for a little earthquake
enough to close
for the afternoon

I can only concur
aware that as senior
I am readily relegated

To the same slot
as a snotty child
prey to wetted pants

My essential tremor
may betoken final ague
or only ordinary use

Her bored beckoning
however sweetened
with synthetic sugar

Is a muffled pile driver
yet it does drill
leaching memory

Flattens my affect
ability to reach out
create new associations

The passing youth
to whom I am invisible
makes more inevitable

Shovelfuls of dirt
flung from my grave
still undug

Their indifference
is the great leveler
of ability even genius

I'm invited even urged
to descend before ready
or even fully ripe

Acknowledgements

Thanks to Todd Swift and Kelly Davio for selecting
and ordering these poems from the thousand or
so I have written since 1980, to create my debut
collection.

⌐ **EYEWEAR** PUBLISHING